Grace & Faith

by Andrew Wommack

Grace & Faith

The Formula for a Balanced Christian Walk

by Andrew Wommack

Grace & Faith

Cover Design by Richard Nakamoto

Printed in the United States of America

ACKNOWLEDGMENTS

I wish to express my appreciation to:

Robert Larson and John Calhoun for their editing expertise;

Dean Jones for proofreading the drafts of *Grace & Faith*;

Cindi Deville for the countless hours spent typing the drafts of *Grace & Faith*;

Mike Martin for his diligence in securing a publisher and for taking care of all the details.

CONTENTS

Grace & Faith

INTRODUCTION

Grace and faith are two of the most important and most taught doctrines of the Bible, and yet, seldom are these two truths combined. In fact, many people view these two forces as opposing each other.

Those who major on grace tend to believe that faith doesn't really matter much: it's all up to God's grace. And likewise, those who are "into faith" don't leave much up to God's grace.

The purpose of this book is to show the relationship between grace and faith and then apply the knowledge we learn to our lives. Only in combining these two powerful truths do we arrive at the truth.

The truths contained in this book will resolve many conflicts, answer many questions, and produce a new understanding of how we receive from God that is guaranteed to enrich our personal relationship with the Lord.

If you have been struggling with faith — if you have had difficulty receiving answers to prayers — this is a message you desperately need. No matter what your condition is when you read this book, remember, I have prayed your heart will be open to the Spirit of God as you read. So read, expecting God to minister to you, and He will!

Andrew Wommack
Colorado Springs, Colorado

Mistaken Faith

1

MISTAKEN FAITH

For thousands of years, a controversy has raged over whether salvation is a sovereign work of God or whether we earn it by our actions. Even among those who agree on what is necessary to obtain salvation, the same question still exists when it comes to maintaining a right relationship with God. Nowhere is this conflict more apparent than when dealing with the subjects of grace and faith. Many people view these as opposing forces. This is even true when we talk about faith and grace. One person will say, "I believe in salvation by grace." Another will say, "I believe in salvation by faith."

But they're both wrong. The Scripture doesn't say we're saved by grace or by faith.

It actually says we're saved by grace through faith.

> "For by grace are ye saved through faith; and that not of yourselves: it is the gift of God: Not of works, lest any man should boast."
>
> Ephesians 2:8, 9

We are not saved by one or the other. We are saved by a combination of the two.

Too often we have a tendency to take a truth from God's Word and focus on it to the exclusion of other biblical truths. And that's how we get into error.

Error is simply truth taken to an extreme or taken as the sole truth. No truth from God's Word stands independent of another truth.

Faith Isn't Alone

As much as I believe in faith, I know preaching faith alone will cause error. If I neglect the truth of love, I can't preach the whole truth about faith. The Bible tells us that faith "worketh by love" (Gal. 5:6). Even if we do all the right things in faith, we will not profit if our actions lack the love of God (1 Cor. 13:1, 3).

We can't just pick and choose what we want from God's Word. We must be able to bring individual truths of God's Word into harmony with the rest of the Bible.

Faith and grace are like sodium and chlorine. Both sodium and chlorine are poisonous. If we consume either one in sufficient quantities, it will kill us. Yet, if we combine the two properly, the result is sodium chloride — or table salt. And salt is something we can't live without!

It's the same with grace and faith. Grace is important, but if we focus on grace to the exclusion of faith, we'll have problems.

In the rural area where I live, we have ditches on both sides of our dirt roads. Driving on those reminds me of how we must balance grace and faith. If you're veering into one ditch, the tendency is to pull on the steering wheel to get out of that ditch. But if you're not careful, you'll veer too far in the opposite direction and hit the other ditch.

That's what happens with truth from God's Word. If we're discovering God's grace and are so excited about it we forget the other truths of the Word, we might "hit the ditch." The proper way is to go right down the middle and avoid the ditches. We must balance these truths. We can't choose either grace or faith.

And the first step is to think about what grace actually is.

The Grace
We Can't
Earn

2

THE GRACE WE CAN'T EARN

A minister once asked his congregation what grace is and he got a different answer from each person present. Everyone has his own definition of grace, but the most common definition is simply "unmerited favor." That's the literal meaning of the original Greek word, "charis."

"Unmerited favor" means God has done, and will keep doing, things for us regardless of what we have done or what we deserve. Grace is something God gives us freely. It's never based on performance.

God's grace is something He commended toward us "in that, while we were yet sinners, Christ died for us" (Rom. 5:8). Jesus

died for us before we had ever done anything for Him. That's grace!

God's Grace Is Equal for All

Since it is not based on actions, God's
grace is the same to everyone. No matter
how good we are, we get no more grace; no
matter how bad we are, we get no less grace.
Grace is totally dependent on the nature and
character of God — it's not dependent on
our actions. God chose to give us grace no
matter what we deserve. Titus 2:11 tells us,
"For the grace of God that bringeth salvation
hath appeared to all men."

God's grace — the grace that brings salvation — has appeared to all men. That
means it has come to every man, woman,
and child who has ever lived on the face of
the earth. Jesus didn't die just for the people
He knew would become Christians. He died
for the sins of the entire world. In 1 John 2:2
we read, "And he is the propitiation for our
sins: and not for ours only, but also for the
sins of the whole world."

That means the sins of Adolf Hitler were
paid for just as surely as yours or mine. As
far as we know, Hitler didn't receive God's
grace, but God offered it to him just the

same. God made an atonement for every person's sins and He offered that atonement to everyone. No one is beyond the grace of God.

But this does not mean all men are saved. Why? Because grace alone doesn't save.

If grace alone saved, then everyone would be saved. The Scripture says the grace of God which brings salvation has appeared to all men. But grace alone does not release the power of God.

Grace has to be mixed with faith. Faith is our response.

So let's talk about how grace and faith work together in harmony.

Grace
for the
Taking

3

GRACE FOR THE TAKING

People are always asking me, "Why does God do this? Why does God do that? Why didn't God do this instead?"

They don't understand that it's not just up to God to move. Before the power of God can be manifested in our lives, we have to respond to what God has done.

That's a critical truth. Everything is not just up to God. Grace is what God does and faith is what we do. We're part of the process.

Take salvation, for example. God has offered salvation to every person who has ever lived — to every murderer, every rapist, and every coward. But not every person has been saved. Why? Because not every person responds in a positive way to what God has done. Is it God who is sending people to hell? On the contrary, people are sending themselves to hell!

God prepared hell for the devil and his angels (Rev. 20:10). He never intended for people to go there. But people are going there because they have chosen to reject God's grace.

Grace Taught to an Extreme

I've heard some people teach on grace to an extreme. They have told me, "Brother, you don't make God do anything. You have nothing to do with the power of God." I disagree.

One day I was talking with a pastor about a little girl who needed healing. "Look," he said to me, "if God wants to heal her, she's going to be healed whether we pray for her or not. We have nothing to do with God's power on this earth. It's totally up to God's grace."

That, my friend, is the beginning of heresy.

God said believers will "lay hands on the sick, and they shall recover" (Mk. 16:18b). It's God's healing power, but it flows through our hands! Our faith releases with God's grace.

That pastor believed a doctrine called, "the sovereignty of God." The word "sovereign" is not used in the Bible, but the dictionary defines it as meaning "independent." The United States is a sovereign nation. We broke away from Great Britain. We are independent. Great Britain can't tell us what to do. They don't set our laws. But does that mean America is a lawless nation? No, it just means Great Britain does not set our laws.

In the same way, God is sovereign. No one tells Him what to do or how to act. However, this does not mean God has no restrictions.

Can God Be Put in a Box?

I've heard people say, "Well, God is sovereign. You never know what He's going to do. You can't put God in a box."

It is true we can't put God in a box, but we can take Him at His Word. He'll never violate His own Word.

When God said, "This is what I will do,"
He limited Himself (Ps. 89:34; 138:2). God
will not overstep the bounds of what He said
He would do (Num. 23:19). He will not enter
in and do the things He commanded us to
do.

For example, God told us to resist the
devil and the devil will flee from us (James
4:7). But if we don't resist the devil, God
won't do it for us. God, by grace, has given
us authority over the devil, but if we don't
stand up to the devil, mixing God's grace
with our faith, the devil will run right over
us. And it won't be God who let it happen. It
will be we, ourselves, who let Satan run over
us.

When I was about six years old, I at-
tended a church Vacation Bible School along
with 600 other kids. One day, when I was sitting in the back row, the pastor stood up
and waved a dollar bill.

"I'll give this dollar bill to the first child
who comes up here and takes it!" he said.

"Boy, what a bummer!" I thought to myself. "Of all the days to be sitting in the back
row!"

Instantly, 30 or 40 kids were at the front
yelling, "I'll take it! I'll take it!"

But the pastor just stood there holding the dollar bill.

"What's the matter?" I thought to myself. "All of those kids want that dollar bill and he said he'd give it to the first one who would go up and take it."

But the pastor just stood there and repeated what he'd said. Suddenly, it dawned on me what he was saying.

From the back row, I ran down the aisle, pushed through all those kids, climbed up the pastor's side, reached up and grabbed that dollar bill!

That's just like grace. The dollar bill was a gift, but I had to take it. Grace and faith always work together. Faith takes what God has already provided.

Not Grace Alone

I know of denominations that preach salvation is by grace alone. There's even one denomination that believes individuals are predestined to be either saved or damned, which means they have no control over whether they're born again or not. Consequently, this denomination feels little need to witness for Christ. They simply "trust God."

One woman in this particular denomination believed salvation was entirely up to God. Because of that, she never shared the Gospel with her own husband. The man was 60 years old before someone else explained to him the simple truth about salvation.

"I've never heard that," the man said as he began to cry. "You mean I can choose to be saved? I can be born again?"

"Yes!" the other person said.

That 60-year-old man was born again, but thanks only to someone who believed salvation involves a personal choice.

Grace has provided salvation, healing, deliverance, and prosperity for us. God has already done everything for us by grace, but faith is the way we receive it.

When people ask me, "Why is God letting my marriage fall apart? Why has God done this to me?" or "Why did God bring this sickness to me? How could He let this happen?" I say to them, "God didn't make you sick, or unhappy in your marriage." Not at all.

God, by grace, has provided healing for every person who has ever walked the earth (Is. 53:5; Matt. 8:17; 1 Pet. 2:24; 3 John 2). But not everyone is healthy. Why? Because of their own ignorance, rebellion, or for any number of other reasons. God is not the author of their sickness (James 1:13-17).

God's grace is unconditional. He denies it to no one. God's grace is consistent. We can't earn it or lose it because of what we do. God's grace is constant. It never changes.

The only thing that can stop grace from working is our own lack of faith.

But what is faith? In the next few pages, we'll talk about faith and what it means in our lives.

The
"Pry-Bar"
Faith

4

THE "PRY-BAR"
FAITH

According to 2 Peter 1:3 "his divine
power hath given unto us all things that
pertain unto life and godliness, through the
knowledge of him that hath called us to
glory and virtue." Faith is certainly one of
those things, so faith is based on knowledge
— a knowledge of God's Word. Wrong thinking produces wrong believing. We need to
clarify some things in our thinking concern-
ing faith.

Most people think faith is something we
do to gain a response from God. We often
think if we confess the Word of God, then
God will respond and give us what we need.

Or if we pay our tithes or pray, God will give us what we want.

But that's not faith! In fact, it's very close to knocking on wood, as the pagans do! Whenever we rely on what we do instead of God's grace, we are acting just like unbelievers.

Pagan religions proudly say, "Well, I took an oath of poverty: I shaved my head. I fasted. I did this, I did that. So now I know God is going to hear my prayer. God is going to move in my life."

But it's not just pagans who do this.

What Does God Want?

I've had Christians come up to me and say, "Brother, I've been fasting and praying, reading my Bible, going to church, paying my tithes ... what does God want?"

Well, they just showed me what their problem is. They're putting faith in what they've done and not in God's grace. Faith is not something we do to gain God's response.

Although faith has many definitions, my favorite one is that faith is our positive response to God's grace. That simply means faith is our positive response to something God has already done.

I don't confess the Word of God to get God to heal me. I confess "by His stripes I am healed" because I believe it's already true (1 Pet. 2:24). I'm simply speaking what I really believe — I'm not making God heal me.

I've heard people say, "God does nothing until we do something. When we do something, then and only then will God act on our behalf. If we just pray, if we do this or do that, then God will move in our lives."

But that's not faith at all! If we're not having faith in something God has already done totally independent of us, then it's not true biblical faith. It's a belief in works.

Too many people use faith like a pry-bar on God.

"God," they say, "I'm going to confess 589 times and I'm going to do this and I'm going to do that 'til You do something!"

But we won't hear from God when we pray like that.

And it's God's mercy that we hear nothing! Because, in effect, our prayer is saying, "God, give me justice. I deserve this or that."

But we don't need justice! We need mercy!

Mercy — Not Justice

I used to work in a photography studio in Childress, Texas. Sometimes we would have women come in to view their proofs and they would say, "This picture doesn't do me justice." I always want to say, "Lady, you don't need justice. You need mercy!"

If we got justice, we'd all go to hell — every one of us! We deserve absolutely nothing from God based on our merits.

James 4:17 says, "Therefore to him that knoweth to do good, and doeth it not, to him it is sin." Sin is not only the things we have done that are wrong, it's the things we know to do and don't do. We can't earn anything from God based on our goodness and righteousness. And thinking we can is certainly the greatest sin of all!

Brothers and sisters, it's the height of arrogance to think we can use our faith, or anything else, to make God do anything!

All too often, we see this attitude in something we call "intercessory prayer." As important as this is, it's lined with pitfalls which we'll look at in the next chapter.

Why Intercessory Prayer Can't Replace Jesus

5

WHY INTERCESSORY PRAYER CAN'T REPLACE JESUS

When I first became excited about the Lord, I started praying for revival. I was so enthused, I organized all-night prayer meetings to "pray in" a revival. But the longest those "all night" meetings ever lasted was 11:30. This was before I received the Baptism of the Holy Spirit and prayed in tongues. Without that, we prayed for the whole world and every dog in it in less than an hour!

I was so frustrated, I tried to discover what I was doing wrong. I started reading about the great revivals — the Welsh revival, the New Hebrides revival, the Moravian revival, and many others. As I read, I noticed that every revival seemed to start with a group of people who just "grabbed hold of God" and, through prayer, brought revival into being.

I was not alone in my observation. When most people talk about revival, they emphasize prayer. "We're just supposed to pray heaven down," they say as they quote Scriptures like Isaiah 64:1, "Oh that Thou wouldest rend the heavens, that Thou wouldest come down, that the mountains might flow down at Thy presence."

A Wrong Attitude

Because of this, I developed a wrong attitude — an attitude many people share about revival.

I thought God was so put out with the human race that He turned His back on us because we were so ungodly. I pictured God as no longer able to abide dealing with us because we were so depraved and rotten. But one day, I thought, an intercessor would come along and say, "Oh God, have mercy on us! Oh God, please turn around! Oh God, please pour out Your Spirit again!"

And I thought God was up there saying, "Upon a bunch of people like you? You've got to be kidding!"

So the intercessor would keep interceding and saying, "Oh, please, God" until God finally would say, "Well, if you won't leave Me alone, I'll have to do it."

What an attitude! To think God is willing for the world to go to Hell — and the world would go to Hell — if it weren't for these great intercessors who have so much love and compassion for the world!

We think we've got to grab the horns of the altar and shake it until God comes out. We're trying to grab hold of God and not let go until He pours out His blessing!

That's ridiculous! We aren't more concerned about people than God is! We don't have to get God prayed into compassion for people. We don't need to turn God around.

But each of us needs to admit we've tried to do just that. We think, "I don't know why God isn't doing this, but I'm going to grab hold of God through faith and not let go until He gives me what I want!"

No wonder we end up frustrated.

We can't make God do anything.

Intercessory Prayer

Knowing this, we can see the wrong attitudes that have crept into the ministry we call "intercessory prayer."

Of course I believe in intercessory prayer. But I also think it's potentially one of the most dangerous ministries in the church today. I personally know of four churches that were split through intercessory prayer groups.

Most intercessors I've known are prideful people. They think they've grabbed hold of God and they're the ones making the church work! They think they're the ones keeping everything in line! They may sound humble and say, "Oh, we're nothing. It's all the Lord," but at the same time they're thinking, "We are the ones who grabbed hold of God and made Him do these things through our intercession."

But intercession can't make God do anything. We don't need to change God's mind. We don't need to motivate God. We don't need to beg, bawl, and plead with God. The New Testament shows us a completely different way of intercession.

New Testament Intercession

The New Testament intercessor doesn't fight with God. He's not wrestling with the Almighty. He's simply putting faith in God's grace.

The New Testament intercessor says, "Father, thank You! I know You've already poured out Your Spirit. The promise is unto us, and unto our children, and unto them that are afar off, even as many as the Lord our God shall call (Acts 2:39). But Satan is standing against this. Satan, religion, tradition — they're binding people today! Father, people's eyes are blind! I break the power of this blindness!"

The New Testament intercessor doesn't have to ask God for anything. He's searching the mind of God and commanding the devil to back off and let God's will come to pass! He's binding the demonic spirits who are holding people in bondage.

And it's fun and exciting to go in and execute the judgment God has already sent upon the devil and then praise God for it. Hallelujah! Praise is a powerful form of intercession! (Matt. 21:16 with Ps. 8:2 NIV).

But intercession in the Old Testament was different. In Exodus, Moses told God to repent (32:11-13) and God actually did (vs. 14). Moses changed God's mind (Ps. 106:23). People use this example and the example of Abraham bargaining with God to spare the cities of Sodom and Gomorrah (Gen. 18:22, 23) to contend that intercessors are supposed to turn God from His fierce wrath. But if Moses asked God to repent in the New Testament, he would have been rebuked.

Why? Because Jesus was an intercessor who ended all the earlier types of intercession. Jesus completely pacified the wrath of God. He bore all the punishment. If we try to step into His shoes and be the intermediary, we're completely out of line.

In fact, Jesus' disciples were rebuked for trying to use the Old Testament intercessory ways and do what Elijah did (Lk. 9:51-56). There's a difference between the old covenant and the new covenant.

We can't do what Jesus died to do. All we can do is receive by faith and put faith in what Jesus has already done for us.

That's a powerful truth and when we understand it, everything in the Christian life takes on an entirely different perspective ...

especially our attitudes about faith. Now let's see how easily faith can be confused with other forms of spiritual activity.

Taking
the Struggle
Out of Faith

6

TAKING THE STRUGGLE OUT OF FAITH

Suppose someone, trying to apply Mark 11:24, says, "I confess with my mouth and believe in my heart that I can steal a million dollars and won't be caught. I confess it'll be the perfect bank robbery because I'm using the principles of faith." What will happen? If he tries to rob a bank, he'll probably be caught.

Why? Because faith only appropriates what God has already provided by His own free will. And since God's grace doesn't provide the ability to be a thief, no amount of faith and confessing will make someone a good thief.

This may seem ridiculously obvious, but I've heard people try to do the same thing with other desires they have. They tell themselves, "I confess it with my mouth. I believe I receive when I pray that such-and-such will happen."

I know a woman who claimed a nationally-known minister as her mate in this way. She actually commanded this man's wife to die, because she felt the wife was blocking God's perfect will. She based her thoughts all on Mark 11:24. But of course, operating that way just isn't going to work. Faith can't make it happen, because God didn't provide us with the ability to murder and commit adultery by grace.

Faith Receives

Faith can't bring to pass something God hasn't provided. All faith does is receive what God has already provided. When we understand this, we take all the struggle out of faith.

When most people talk about faith, they're actually talking about works. They're doing things, confessing the Word, and doing this or that — thinking all the while they're going to move God.

If we're pointing toward heaven and saying, "God, we've paid our tithes, we've gone to church, we've done all these things — now You do something," we're not operating in God's kind of faith.

We're into works if we're calling attention to what we have done in order to get God to do something.

We've had a lot of teaching that has really perverted the simplicity of the things of God. All we've really had was religion!

Religion teaches we have to do things to please God. Did you ever wonder why? It's because doing things is advantageous to religion!

Religion wants us to go to church. But religion doesn't say, "Come to church because you love God and other people." Instead, religion says, "If you don't go to church, God won't bless you."

Nonsense! If we never came to church another day in our lives, God would love us the same way He did when He commended his love towards us as sinners (Rom. 5:8). God's grace is consistent toward us even if we never darken the door of a church again for the rest of our lives. Going to church doesn't change God's attitude toward us. It changes our attitude towards God.

God Has Given Everything

God, by grace, has already freely given us everything, including healing. God has already healed every person who will ever get healed. In 1 Peter 2:24 we read, "by whose stripes ye were healed." We can't do anything today to make God heal a person.

But we can do something to receive what God has already given. I recently saw God open a blind eye during a service. But that eye was already healed over 2000 years ago! All we did was reach out by faith and say, "Thank You, Jesus, every need we have is supplied, and we receive it!" And the man began to see out of his blind eye! That man put faith in what Jesus had done and not in his own performance.

It's a good thing, too, because if we waited to be worthy of God's blessing before we have it, we'd never be ready. We could go to church every time the doors were open, pray all night, pay our tithes faithfully, never drink or cuss, and we'd still have areas in our lives that were unworthy.

Sometimes we even try to gain God's approval by fasting. But that, too, can be a roadblock which we'll talk about in "Fasting Doesn't Impress God."

Fasting
Doesn't
Impress
God

7

FASTING DOESN'T IMPRESS GOD

I was in the grocery store recently and saw a little kid stop at the candy shelf. The kid didn't hesitate a minute. He started to scream and yell that he wanted some candy. His mother said no at first, but as the kid kept screaming, I could see her weaken. Finally, she gave in and bought him a candy bar.

Unfortunately, we sometimes treat our heavenly Father just as that kid treated his mother — especially when it comes to fasting.

Too often we use fasting as a last resort to convince God to do what we want. First we pray, confess, study the Word, and get agreement from somebody else. But if that doesn't work, we say, "Bless God, I'm going to go on a fast and I'm not going to come off until I receive from God."

What we're really thinking is, "When I begin to look pitiful, I know, God, You're going to be moved with compassion. You're going to look at me starving, and I don't care how mad You are, I know it's going to turn You around."

The idea is to play on God's mercy when all else fails.

But God isn't impressed. Fasting doesn't give us any extra points with God. God's not moved by fasting. Fasting does nothing for God. If faith in the name of Jesus won't get it, fasting won't get it either.

Why Fast?

So why fast? Because fasting changes us!

When we're having problems and we've already prayed and released our faith and done everything we know to do and we still haven't seen any results, the problem is not God's failure to respond. By grace, God has already provided for us. But Satan is stopping us from receiving what God has for us. Most of the time he uses things inside of us to do it — things such as feelings like fear, doubt, and discouragement.

When we fast, we put a spotlight on carnal desires. Our flesh rebels during a fast if it has not been brought into subjection. Every carnal reaction and emotion rises to the surface.

We hear people give testimonies about fasting and say, "I went on a 21 day fast and saw three angels and five visions, heard God speak to me in an audible voice, and received divine direction for the next 10 years!"

We say, "Hey, I like that. I think I'll go on a 21 day fast!" By noon on the first day we've got a headache and we're saying, "Hey, this isn't what I was expecting! This isn't like the 700 Club testimony! I'm quitting this fast!"

Very seldom do we see three angels, five visions, or hear the audible voice of God. I've never had a fast like that and I don't care if I ever do. That's not the purpose of a fast. The true purpose of a fast is to deal with our flesh — those carnal reactions and emotions that rise to the surface every time we start denying our flesh.

A True Fast

A true fast is not only a fast from food, it's a fast from everything in our daily lifestyle. We are focusing our attention completely on God and our flesh cries out. "I can't forget how bad that person treated me," our flesh might protest. And right away, we become aware of at least one thing that's blocking the grace God wants us to receive from Him.

Food is the strongest desire of our flesh — people have murdered for food — and it shows us our carnality very clearly.

Our body will complain, "Give me food!" But we answer, "Body, we don't live by bread alone, but by every word that proceeds out of the mouth of God!" (Matt. 4:4)

"Oh, yeah?" our body answers. "I want something to eat and I want it right now!"

"Look body," we say, "You're not going to rule me! My spirit is going to rule! And if you keep troubling me, we're going to go some extra days!"

Pretty soon our body becomes quiet. Our body submits and our spirit gains power. And when we get off our fast, we're stronger than horseradish! God hasn't given us extra

---

power; we just broke the hold our flesh had on us. Our spirit has more control than it has ever had over us.

Now when we pray we get answers!

But did our fast make God do something?

No, our fast didn't impress God at all. It didn't change Him at all. Our fast changed us.

Some people have read Matthew 17:21, "Howbeit this kind goeth not out but by prayer and fasting," and have said that some demons respond only to our prayer and fasting. But Mark 16:17 tells us it is the authority of Jesus' name and our faith in Him that casts out demons. If that won't cast out the devil, neither will our prayers and fasting. Matthew 17:21 actually refers back to the unbelief mentioned in verse 20. It's unbelief that can only be changed by prayer and fasting!

Faith, combined with anything other than God's grace, is not biblical faith. And putting faith in something like fasting will lead to the ultimate in discouragement because it just won't work. We'll end up thinking, "Well, God sure didn't do a thing!"

But the truth is, He has already done everything He is going to do. We just can't re-

ceive what He has done when we're putting
faith in our own efforts.

Of course, we all have difficulty sometimes in receiving what God has already
done for us. In the next few pages, I want to
talk about one of my biggest obstacles in receiving from God. You see, I kept looking at
myself and asking, "Lord, am I worthy?" The
answer, as you will read, was a loud "No" —
and Satan used this resounding response to
load me down with guilt and discouragement.

God,
It's Got
to Be You!

8

GOD, IT'S GOT TO BE YOU!

The first church meeting I ever held was a three-night series. I had never ministered before and I felt intimidated and unsure of myself. I prepared and prayed and worried about those meetings. I had three sermons all ready, one for each night, but on the first night when I got up to minister, I was so shaken up, I preached all three sermons in the first five minutes. There I was with two full nights left to go and nothing to say. I was petrified! I even vowed to God I'd never preach again.

"God," I said, "I embarrassed You and me both tonight!"

Part of my nervousness came because I realized the seriousness of the ministry. I knew I had a responsibility for people's lives if I started ministering. That's when I began to think, "God, I don't know if I'm worthy to do this."

The Performance Trap

That led me straight into the performance trap. I started trying to perform. I made a promise I'd fast at least two weeks before each time I ministered. (Fortunately, I wasn't ministering very much then — I'd starve to death today with that approach!) I would pray for hours. I'd intercede.

But it all profited me nothing! My attitude was wrong. I was fasting to earn the blessings of God! I was saying, "God, I'll do this; now You do something!"

During those days I thought I was doing many good things, but they profited me nothing. I had the wrong attitude..

First Corinthians 13:3 says, "And though I bestow all my goods to feed the poor, and though I give my body to be burned, and have not charity, it profiteth me nothing." Just as with giving, the wrong attitude will cause all of our good works to profit nothing.

However, even though I was a total failure, I couldn't stop ministering. I lived Jeremiah 20:9. "But His word was in mine heart as a burning fire shut up in my bones, and I was weary with forbearing, and I could not stay."

I couldn't stop ministering. I asked God to forgive me for failing. Believing He would help me, I tried again. I did this for over a year.

Something to Share?

Joe Nay, a friend of mine, was holding services, and Jamie and I would go to hear him. Right in the middle of the service, Joe would yell out at me, "Andy, do you have something to share?"

I was spending at least 16 hours a day in the Word and God was giving me revelation knowledge. Tremendous things were happening in my life.

But my first thought when Joe called out was, "Oh, no! I haven't had time to prepare! I haven't thought about how I'm going to say it!"

But I couldn't keep silent so I'd just say, "God, it's got to be YOU!"

I'd stand up and the Word flowed out of me. The gifts of the Spirit would be manifested and people would get delivered and Joe would have to grab the microphone away from me!

Afterward I'd think, "God, this doesn't make sense. I didn't prepare. I didn't do anything. It just flows! The more I pray, the more I fast, the more I prepare, the worse I do! My ministry is being ruined by study and prayer! What's wrong?"

God began to show me I was putting faith in what I had done. But when Joe called on me, I was forced to put my faith totally in Jesus. Without Him, I didn't have a chance. With my faith in Jesus, everything flowed.

When I realized how I was thinking, I told God I'd never prepare for another message in my life. And I never have. If you ask me the topic I'll be ministering on five minutes before I preach, I probably won't be able to tell you. Now notes and planning help most people, but for me, they became my substitute for depending on God.

Preparing The Messenger

I'm not saying you can live carnally and then get up before people and expect God to just flow through you. Whatever you are full of is what will come out (Matt. 12:34) and if you're not full of God's Word, something else will come out. I prepare constantly, but I don't prepare for a particular message. I prepare the messenger instead. And when the messenger is prepared, the message is always ready.

Now I can minister at the drop of a hat and drop my hat to get to minister, because I'm full of the Word.

I've learned to put faith in God and now I'm ready when the devil comes to me and says, "You sorry old thing, Andy. You haven't studied, you haven't prayed, you haven't done so-and-so! What makes you think God can use you?"

I used to try and justify myself based on what I had done, but now, when the devil condemns me, I agree quickly. I just shout, "GUILTY! I really don't deserve a thing! Praise God for Jesus!"

That's what the Bible says, "Agree with thine adversary quickly ... " (Matt. 5:25).

I've learned you never win a victory over the devil by trying to justify yourself.

I remember preparing for a service once in my early days of ministry. I had prayed and studied 16 hours and fasted all day long. I had even read the New Testament through one-and-a-half times in one day! As I was getting ready for the service, I was saying to myself, "Praise God, I've fasted, I've prayed, and I've read the New Testament today!"

I was very pleased, but then the devil came up to me and said, "You've been up for 17 hours; you wasted an entire hour."

I felt so much condemnation, I actually ended up crying out to God, "Oh, God, how can You use me? I've blown a whole hour today! I'm so unworthy!"

Now, when the devil says something like that to me, I just tell him who Jesus is instead of who I am. When I pray for someone, I won't tell him or her how spiritual I've been today. I just pray for him in the name of Jesus and talk about what Jesus did instead of what I've done.

In 1978, I pastored a small church in Pritchett, Colorado. In addition to that, I led five Bible studies a week in the surrounding area. I became so busy ministering to others that I didn't have any time to minister to myself.

One day I promised the Lord that I would fast, study the Word, and pray all day. However, that day I had more people call me for help than ever before.

One man in particular, who I had been witnessing to for a long time, came by and wanted to take me out for lunch. I felt this was a good opportunity, so I went with him and ate twice as much as I normally did.

On my way to Bible study that evening, I felt terrible. "I didn't keep a single one of my promises to You today," I told the Lord. "I don't see how You can use me to minister to anyone tonight."

Out of desperation, I asked the Lord to use me in spite of how miserable I was for the sake of the people who would be at the Bible study. Then I said, "Just do it because of Jesus!"

The Lord replied, "Who did you think I was going to do it because of?"

I had to stop and think. I had anticipated the Lord using me that night because of my fasting, prayer, and Bible study. Since I had failed, my faith had failed. But Jesus hadn't

failed, there's great freedom in that. I would
just tell the people about Jesus and how
faithful He is. I wouldn't even mention what
a failure I was. It worked! The Lord moved in
a miraculous way.

The devil can't corner me anymore. As
Kenneth Copeland has said, "The devil can't
corner me; I'm in the round house now!" No
corners! I've taken away all of Satan's op-
portunities.

Now let's talk some more about this performance trap and how we can find victory
over this subtle intrusion into our walk with
God.

The
Performance
Trap

9

THE PERFORMANCE TRAP

When George Washington accepted his appointment as Commander-in-Chief of the Colonial forces, he said, "I beg it may be remembered by every gentleman in the room that ... I do not think myself equal to the command I am honored with."

Such honesty is rare today, especially in the world's system of worshiping at the shrine of performance. We've been taught we need to do things if we want people to like us.

Parents use this tactic with their children. They say things like, "Johnny, what are your friends going to think if you don't stop sucking your thumb?"

They may be able to stop Johnny sucking his thumb that way, but they're also instilling inside Johnny a fear of people's rejection.

Peer Pressure

I once visited a Christian school that had over 500 students. In the school's brochure, they boasted they used "positive peer pressure" and that's why their school was so good for children. Admittedly, positive peer pressure works.

But students were learning to do whatever it took to be accepted. And when they left the positive peer pressure and went to another school or joined the Army, they suddenly found themselves around negative peer pressure.

This same training, unfortunately, became the vehicle to cause them to get into drugs, sex, and a dozen other sinful things in order to gain acceptance of others.

The whole idea of doing things so others will like us is one we must change as we approach God.

God simply doesn't operate on that system. He doesn't love us and respond to us based on our performance.

I've learned that when I blow it, I can run to God. Instead of feeling guilty and running away from God, I now know it's all right to run right to God in the midst of my worst sin (Heb. 4:16).

And I can just praise Him for His mercy! No matter how badly I blow it, I know I can count on the goodness of God.

God's Goodness

Every person I know who has been mightily used of God has grabbed hold of this truth — God's goodness is greater than their failures.

Some people with great miracle ministries have severe problems. I worked with a person once who had one of the most miraculous ministries seen in recent years.

Some would think the person would have to be a saint for all of those miracles to occur.

But, the closer I got to him, the more I could see he was extremely carnal, harsh with people, cruel, and even unforgiving.

"Now, brother," some would say, "I just don't believe God could use a dirty vessel like that."

Unfortunately, God has no other kind of vessel to use! Each of us has something wrong in his or her life. God has never had a qualified person working for Him yet.

But God uses us in spite of who we are!

Looking for Something Special

I remember the first time I saw someone raised from the dead in my ministry. Now I had been believing God and confessing for years about seeing people raised from the dead.

I guess I thought something special would happen to me at the same time, too. I figured I would somehow no longer feel hungry or tired or inadequate.

Just before church service one day a man approached me and asked me to go with him to pray for his father who had just died. We saw God raise the man from the dead, but when I returned to the service, I actually "bombed out." Not only was I no better, I was terrible!

I went home tired, hungry, and frustrated.

Things hadn't gone as I'd expected. I thought I was supposed to be different after seeing such a great miracle, but I was the same old me.

What a disappointment!

I learned then and there that God didn't use me because of who I was. He used me in spite of who I was!

Fortunately, sin in our lives doesn't keep us from God. God doesn't look at our performance the way people do. And it's a good thing because God's standard is absolute perfection.

He doesn't grade on a curve.

We can score 99 per cent with God and we still fail the test!

God's Law

God's law is like the big window in your living room. You can either drive a truck through the window or shoot a BB through it — it doesn't matter.

Either way the window is broken and needs to be replaced.

God's law isn't 1,000 different commandments. It's one law made up of thousands of components that are all tied together.

James 2:10 says, "For whosoever shall keep the whole law, and yet offend in one point, he is guilty of all."

Even though I have never smoked a cigarette, or said a swear word, or taken an alcoholic drink, I am as guilty before God as an adulterer or a murderer.

God doesn't grade our sins as small or big. Any sin, no matter how small we think it is, separates a lost man from God as surely as the greatest sin we can imagine.

But, praise God, His grace is greater than all of our sins. Romans 5:20 says that where sin abounds, grace abounds greater.

Sin doesn't harden God's heart towards us — it hardens our hearts toward God (Heb. 3:13).

Sin defiles us

Sin keeps us from believing in the goodness of God. Sin defiles our conscience and fills us with guilt that keeps us from God. So, as much as we can, we are called to live holy lives.

But when we fail, we can stand strong in the assurance of God's grace, knowing it's our Lord Jesus and not our performance that makes us acceptable to God.

This truth will set us free! That's good news! So let's talk about other ways we can see more of God's boundless grace.

Relax
and Let God
Bless You

10

RELAX AND LET GOD BLESS YOU

An agnostic once said that it's quite impossible these days to believe in any book, like the Bible, whose authority is unknown. A Christian standing near him asked if the person who had compiled the multiplication table was known.

"Why, no," the agnostic answered.

"Then, of course, you don't believe in it?" the Christian continued.

"Oh, yes, I believe it because it works so well."

"So does the Bible," the Christian said and the agnostic had no answer.

The Bible does work! That's why even
though I know God doesn't love me any
more because I do so, I spend much time
studying the Word of God.

I know the Word contains the truth and
the truth will set me free just like it says in
John 8:32.

The truth doesn't change God; it sets me
free.

It's the same with prayer. I don't pray to
God to impress Him. I pray to be in com-
munion with God. Prayer blesses me and
helps me.

It's the same with fasting and tithing. I
don't do either with the hope that God will
give me extra blessings. I fast to change myself, and I tithe because I love God.

God's Grace Is Constant

God's grace is constant regardless of what
we do. God's grace is the same whether we
go to church or pray or read the Bible or
tithe. God's grace doesn't change depending
on our performance.

But this doesn't mean we can live like the
devil and expect it not to hurt us. The way
we live affects our faith because faith comes
by hearing the Word of God.

We need to read the Bible and pray, but we need to know we don't do it to earn God's love.

When we come to God trying to earn His love, we must disappoint Him since without faith, it is impossible to please God (Heb. 11:6).

It's the same as if one of my children came to me and asked for a dollar. But, instead of just asking, he said, "Dad, you've got to give me a dollar. I've swept the garage and done this or that. You owe me a dollar; now give it to me!"

I know I wouldn't like that at all. My child isn't going to get my response by demanding that I do things.

That's the same reason we see so many problems in marriages today.

Before a couple gets married, they will say, "Honey, would you please do so and so?"

After marriage, the demands start and then we wonder why everyone is so upset. We don't like people to command us to do things — and I can guarantee God doesn't like it either.

The Two Together

We cannot make God do anything. And unless we realize this, we will never receive from God, because it's only by grace through faith that we receive.

It's not God's grace without our faith that works. And it's not our faith without God's grace. It's the two working together in harmony.

That's why many people today who do all the right things, don't receive from God. They're putting their faith in their own efforts instead of God's grace. And without God's grace, we are all destitute.

Apart from God's grace, we wouldn't have anything — not even faith. God is the one who gives us our faith; it's not something we generate ourselves (Eph. 2:8). God actually had to give us faith so we could be born again.

And once we decide to operate in faith, God's faith flows through us.

A few years ago, I was ministering in Ohio. We had packed about 650 people into a church that seats 500 and we had seen some exciting things happen. As the minister was introducing me, I realized that I hadn't even asked God yet what I was going to minister about.

I hadn't thought about it or worried about it. I smiled as I recalled those early days when I was so paranoid about ministering. Now, I minister by God's ability and I just trust Him. And I love to minister! I get blessed from it. It invigorates me.

I've learned that if we're struggling in the things of God — doing all we can and asking God to bless our efforts — we're doing it all wrong. We need to start trusting in Jesus and putting faith in what He has done.

Life-Changing Truth

I can't tell you how important this one truth is. One thing I can say, though, is that it can change your life, as it has already changed my life and the lives of thousands.

A woman in Kansas City with severe emotional problems was given a copy of this message and it completely changed her life. She was so tormented by guilt — thinking she had failed so badly that God could no longer bless her — that she was committed to a mental hospital. But when she understood this truth and really believed it, she became a new person. Today she's a beautiful example of faith in God's grace and she ministers whenever she gets the chance!

God is no respecter of persons. If He can use this message to restore a woman in a mental hospital, He can certainly free you today from your fears and frustrations!

It's torture to try to serve God through our efforts. We need a Savior! We can't be our own Savior!

We can't work hard enough, pray long enough, fast enough, or give enough money in tithes to ever make ourselves acceptable to God. Once we realize that, we can have peace, resting securely in what Jesus has done for us. So, if you feel beaten down because nothing in your life seems to work, just relax. Stop trying, and start trusting.

Open your arms to what God has already given you and let God bless you the way He wants to — and has already done.

He's just waiting for you to receive what He has already provided.

Believe me, your life will change and you will be set free.

ANDREW WOMMACK

Andrew Wommack was brought up in a Christian home in Arlington, Texas, and made a total commitment of his life to the Lord at a very early age. But it was not until he received the Baptism of the Holy Spirit as a teen-ager that he began to experience the power of God in his life.

Since that time, he has served as pastor of three churches in progressive steps to the ministry that God has called him to: teaching the entire body of Christ the "Good News" of our New Testament relationship with Jesus Christ.

Andrew is fulfilling this calling as he travels throughout the nation sharing the simple truths of God's Word with people of various backgrounds. He is heard on radio stations across the country and has distributed over 1,000,000 cassette tapes free of charge.

As a result of seeking God with a pure heart, Andrew has been given revelation knowledge and anointing to present great truths from God's Word with simplicity and clarity. Andrew desires to share these life-changing truths with you.

ORDER FORM

Please add my name to your mailing list and send me more information about Andrew Wommack Ministries.

PLEASE PRINT:

NAME_____

ADDRESS_____

CITY_____

STATE_____

ZIP_____

PHONE_____

MAIL TO:

Europe:
Andrew Wommack Ministries of Europe
P.O. Box 35
Coventry, CV32TP
ENGLAND

All others:
Andrew Wommack Ministries, Inc.
P.O. Box 3333
Colorado Springs, CO 80934-3333